Point of Grace

Winter Wonderland

Point of Grace
Winter Wonderland

As recorded by Point of Grace on Word CD #080688641320

ORIGINAL ARRANGEMENTS AND ORCHESTRATIONS
BY CARL MARSH

TRANSCRIBED BY BRYCE INMAN
EDITED BY BRYCE INMAN & KEN BARKER

CONTENTS

It's the Most Wonderful Time of the Year

Words and Music by
EDWARD POLA and GEORGE WYLE
Arranged by Carl Marsh

par - ties for host - ing, marsh - mal - lows for toast - ing and car - ol - ing out in the

snow. There'll be scar - y ghost sto - ries and tales of the glo - ries of

Ensemble:

Scar - y sto - ries of

Christ - mas - es long, long a - go.

long a - go.

Winter Wonderland

DICK SMITH

FELIX BERNARD
Arranged by Carl Marsh

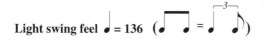

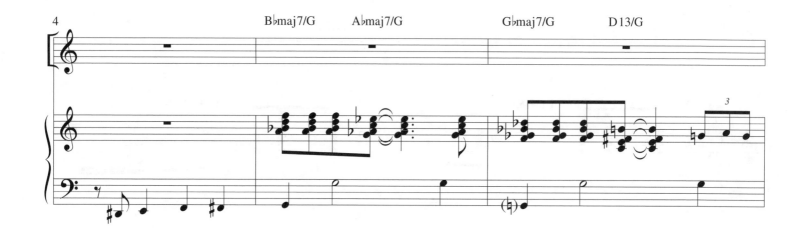

When it snows,_____ it's so

we're go - in' walk - in' in a win - ter won - der - land!

Let There Be Light

Words and Music by
SCOTT KRIPPAYNE
and MARIE REYNOLDS
Arranged by Carl Marsh

Star of won-der, star of night,

star with roy-al beau-ty bright,

west-ward lead-ing, still pro-ceed-ing,

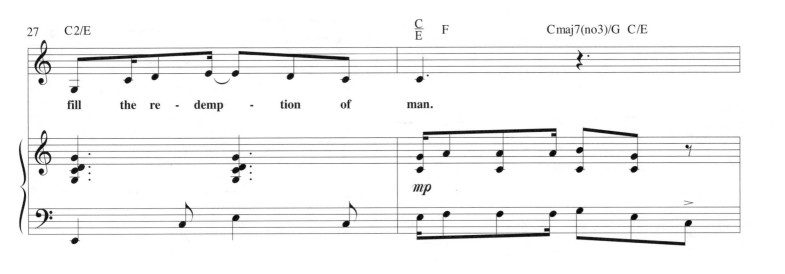

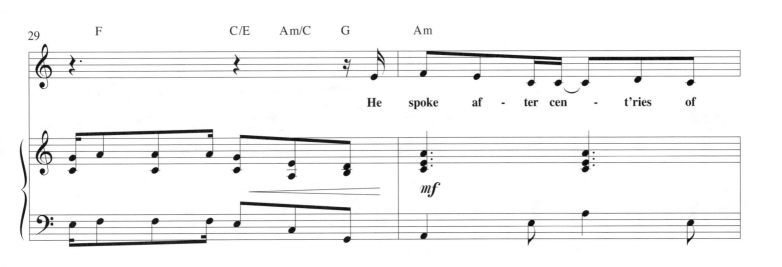

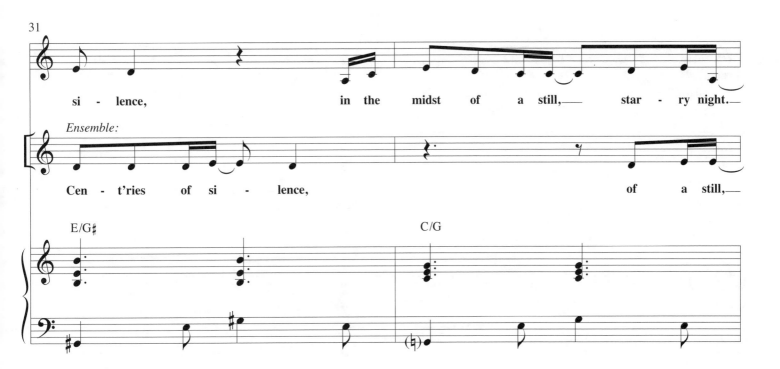

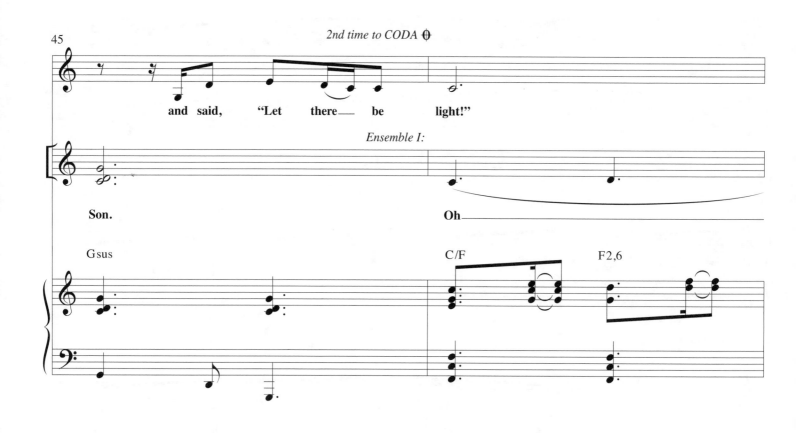

and said, "Let there — be light!"

Son.

Oh—

Gsus   C/F   F2,6

Let there be light!—

Oh—   Oh—

C/F   F2,6   C/F   F2,6   C/F   F2,6

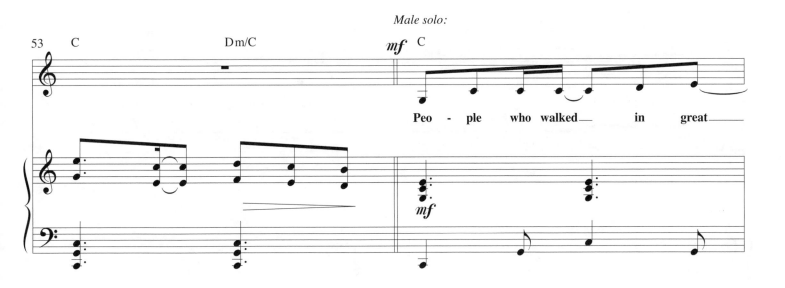

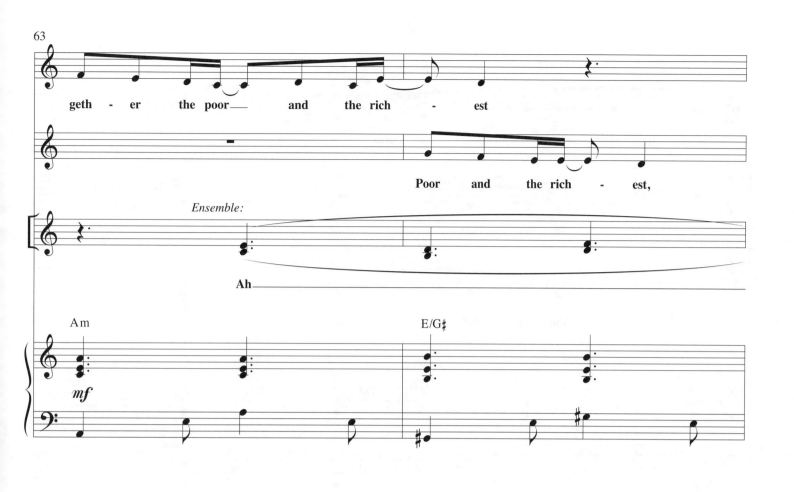

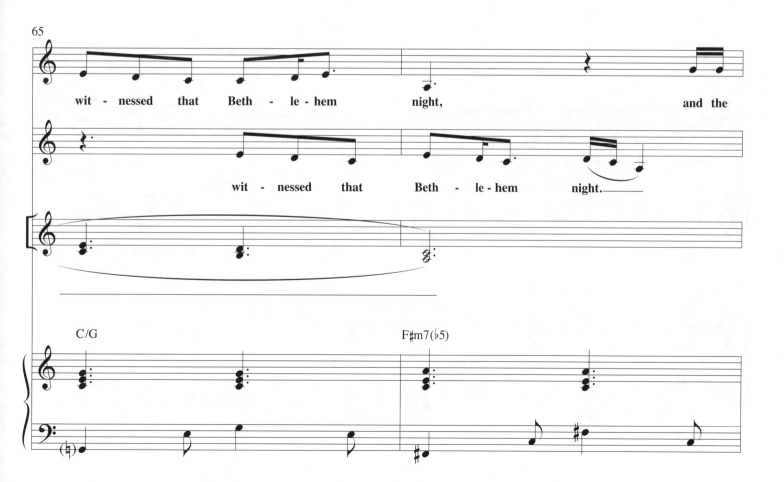

sky full of an - gels an - nounc - ing the

The sky full of an - gels.

The sky full of an - gels.

F2(no3)

C/E

D.S. al CODA 𝄋

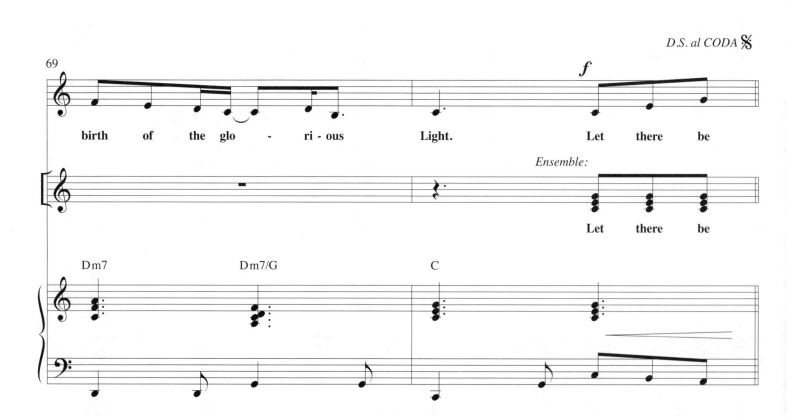

birth of the glo - ri - ous Light. Let there be

Ensemble:

Let there be

Dm7

Dm7/G

C

𝆑

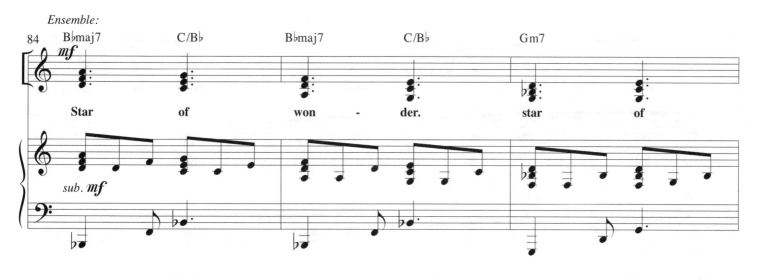

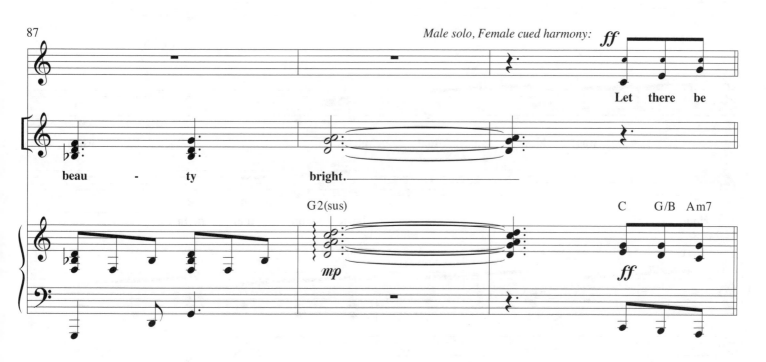

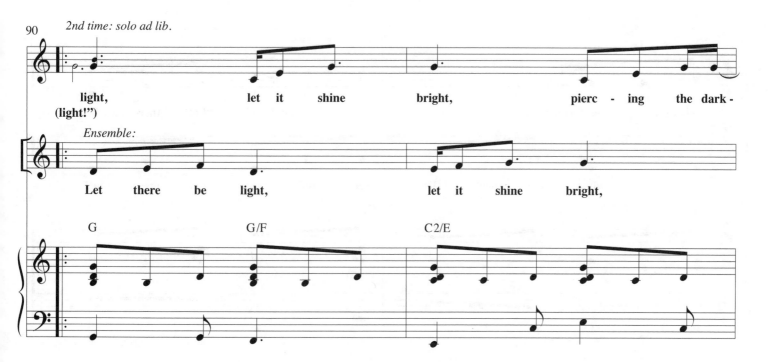

Jingle Bells

Words and Music by
JOHN PIERPONT
Arranged by Carl Marsh

Oh, what fun it is to ride in a one - horse o - pen sleigh!

Big band swing ♩ = 128

ff

B/A   A13   A♯dim7

G♯m/B   Am/C   C♯13   E(♭9)/G   Cmaj7(♯5)/F♯   B7/C♯   C9(♯11)   F♯m7/B

dim.

Straight eighths ♩ = 132

mf

58

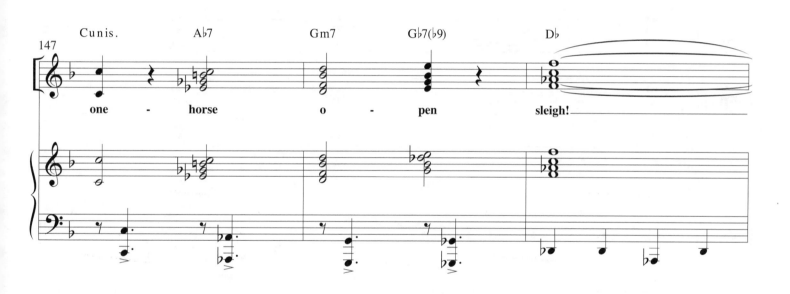

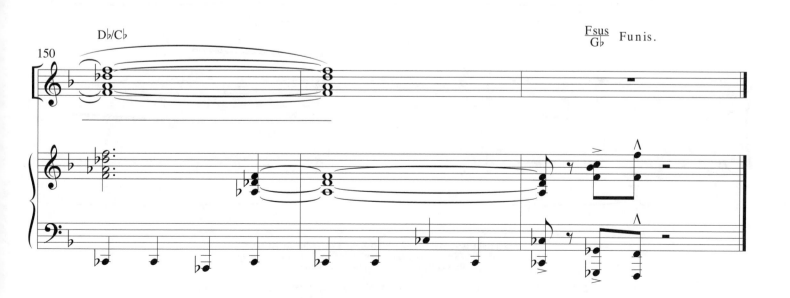

Breath of Heaven
(Mary's Song)

**Words and Music by
CHRIS EATON and AMY GRANT**
Arranged by Carl Marsh

Somberly ♩ = 108   (♩ = ♩ throughout)

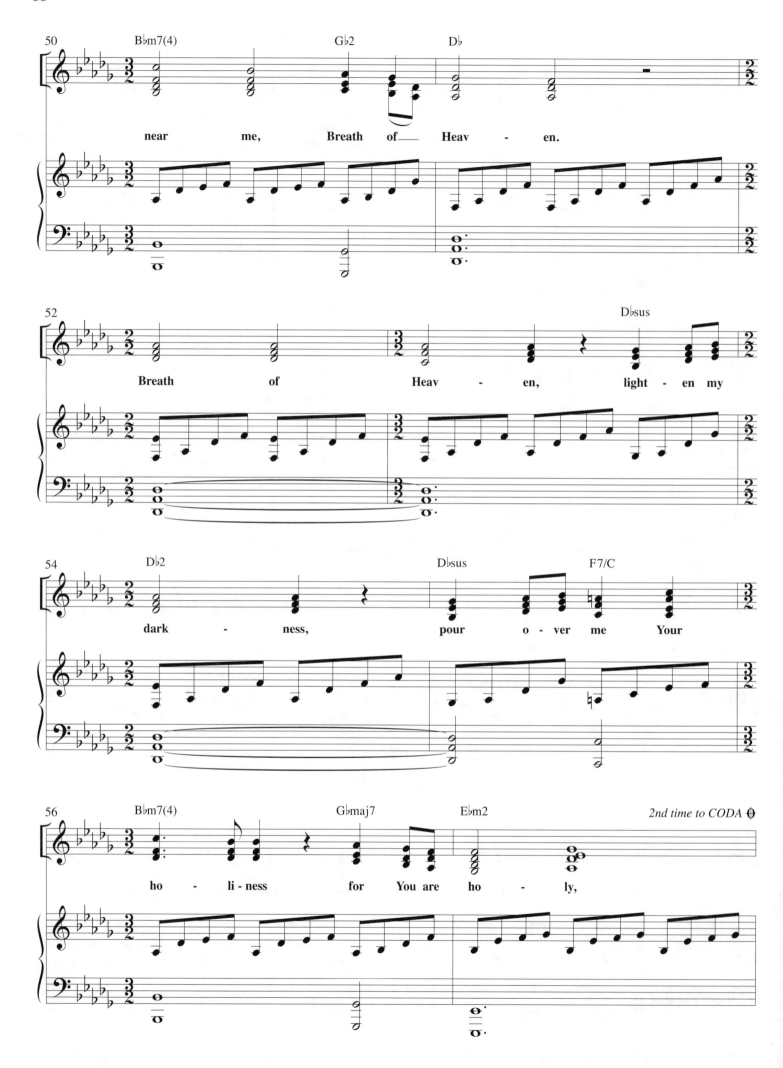

67

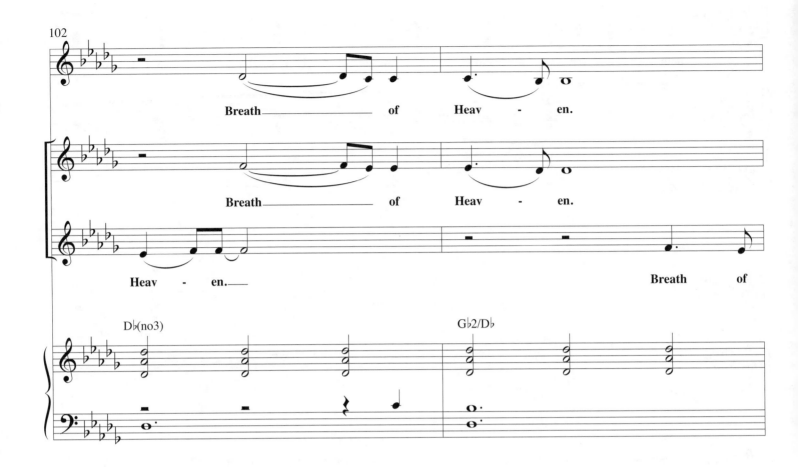

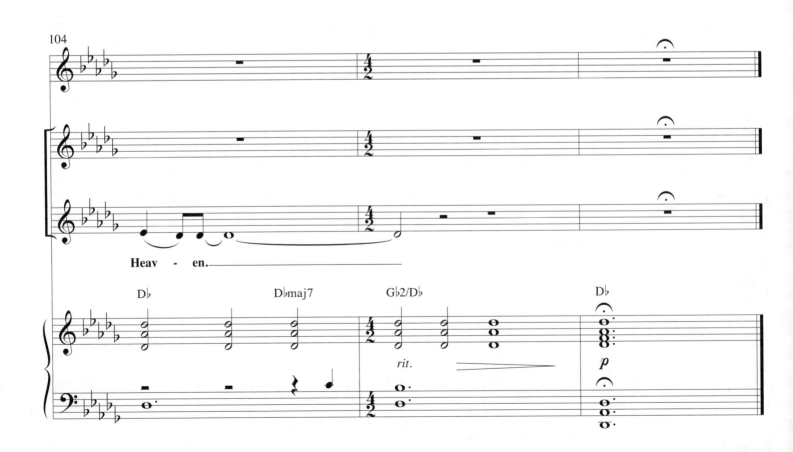

In the First Light

Words and Music by
BOB KAUFLIN
Arranged by Tim Davis

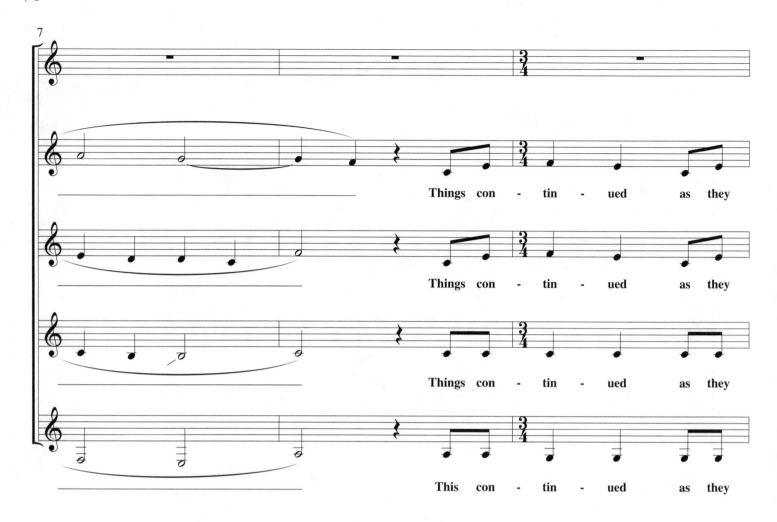

Things con - tin - ued as they

Things con - tin - ued as they

Things con - tin - ued as they

This con - tin - ued as they

While a new - born soft - ly cried.

had been, while a new - born. Ooo

had been, new - born soft - ly cried.

had been, new - born. Ooo

had been, new - born. Ooo

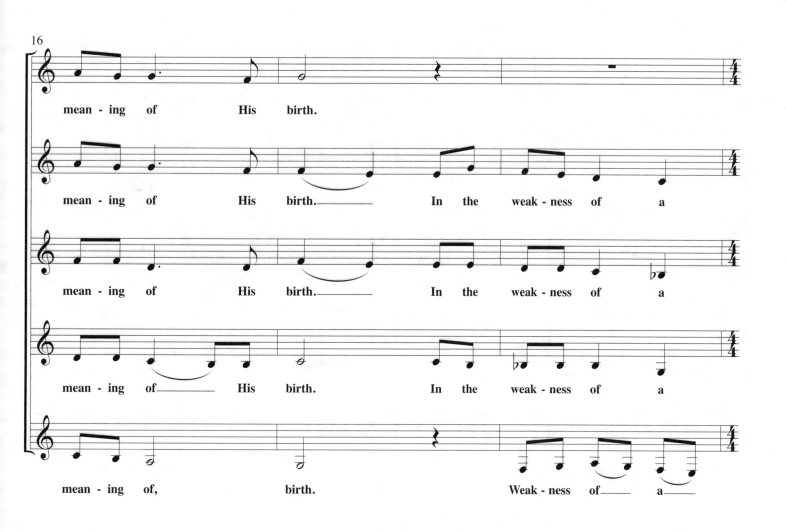

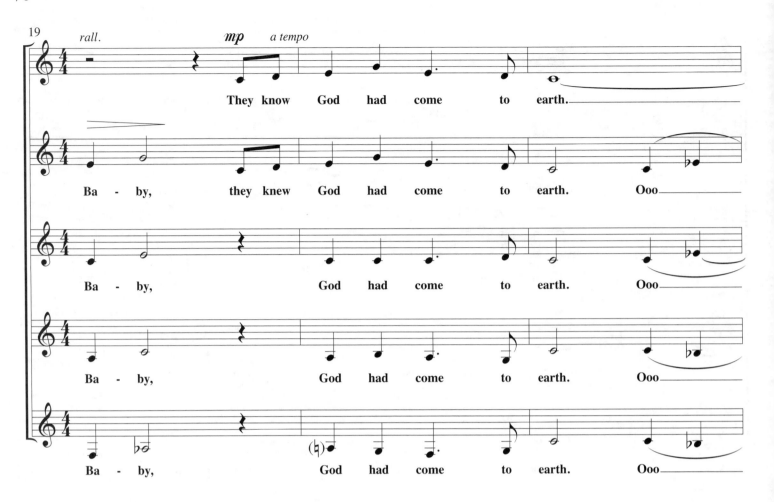

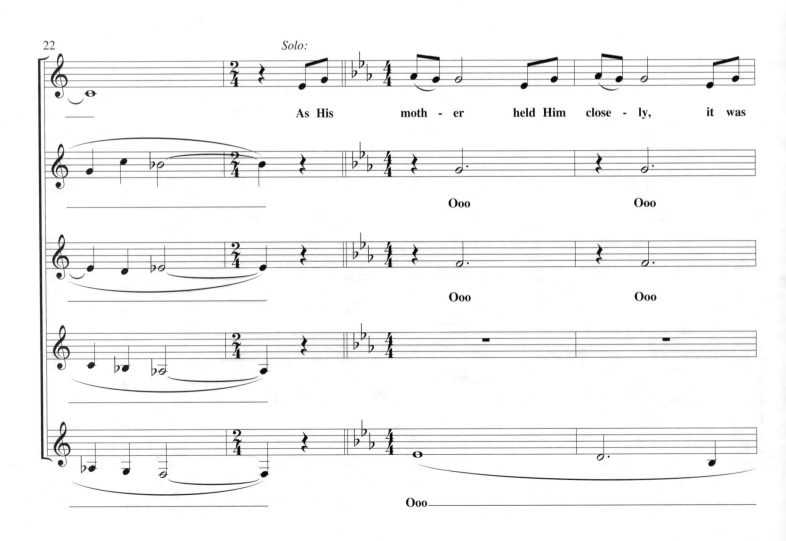

they would nail Him to a tree.

they would nail Him to a, Ooo

they would nail Him to a, Ooo

Ooo

Ooo

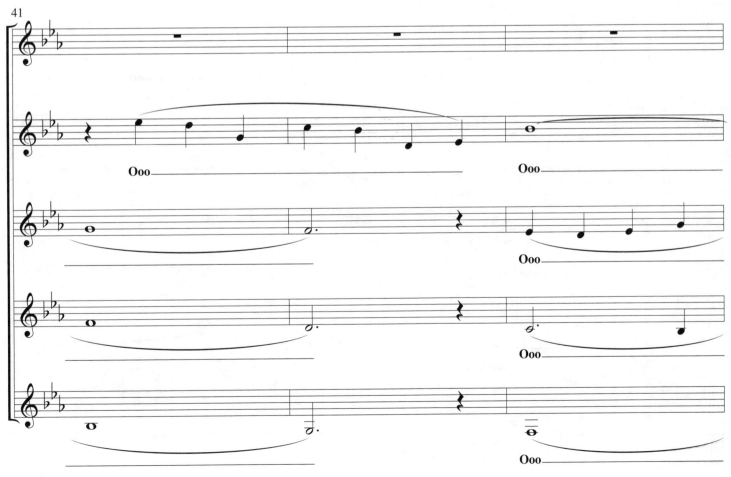

Ooo Ooo

Ooo

Ooo

Ooo

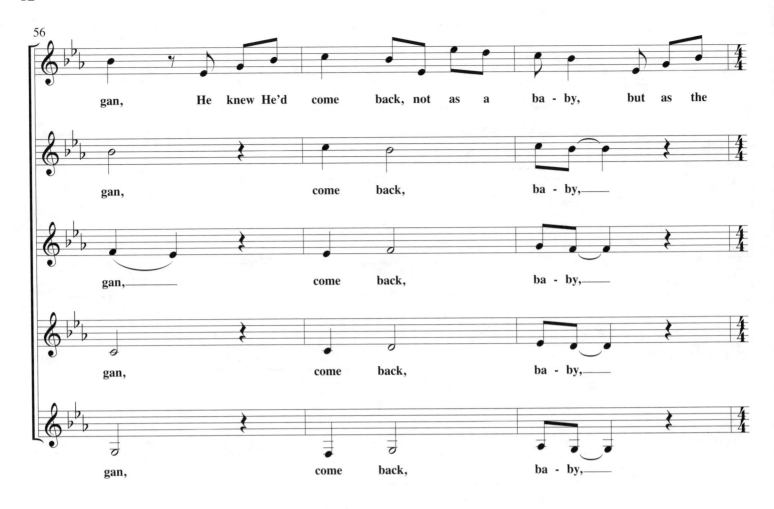

sing - ing on the morn - ing of His birth. But how much

Morn - ing of His birth.

Morn - ing of His birth.

Morn - ing of His birth.

Morn - ing of His birth.

great - er will the song be when He comes a - gain to

Ha Comes a - gain to

Ha Comes a - gain to

Ha Comes a - gain to

Ha Comes a - gain to

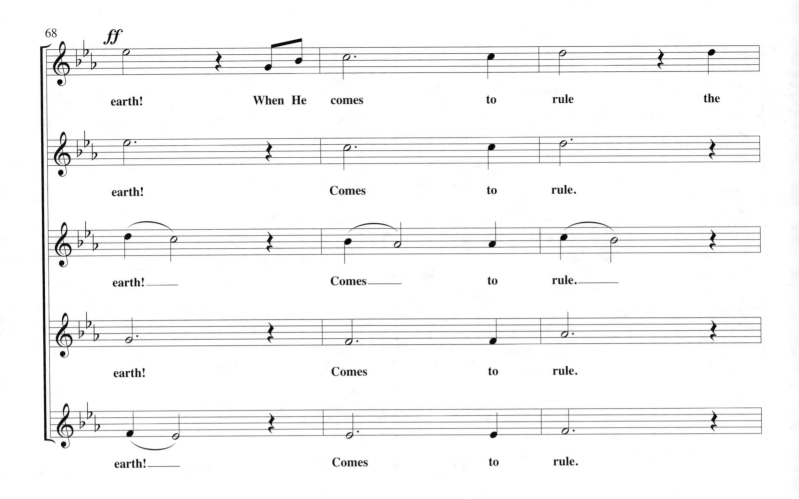

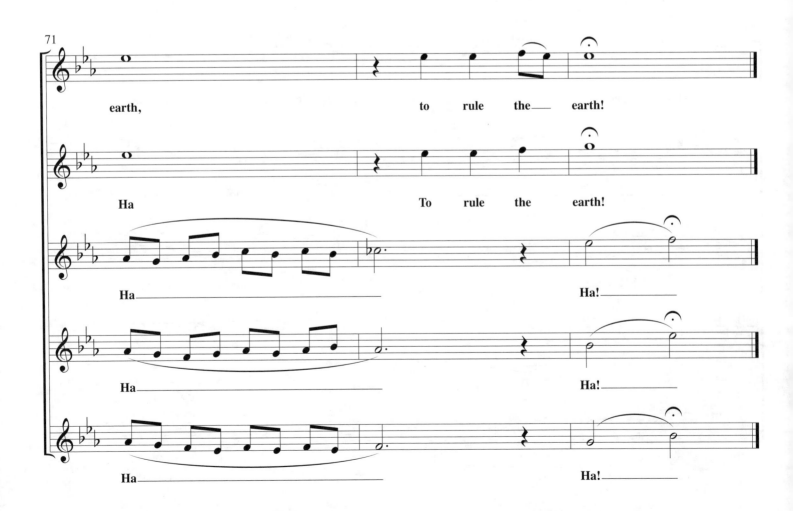

Santa Medley

Arranged by Carl Marsh

Light swing feel ♩ = 88 (swing sixteenths)

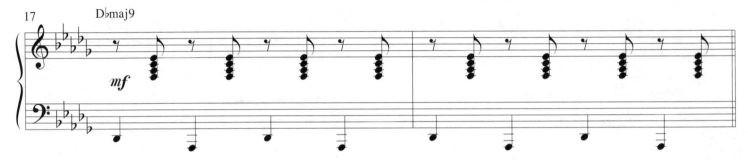

"Here Comes Santa Claus (Right Down Santa Claus Lane)" - Gene Autry and Oakley Haldeman

Here comes San - ta Claus, here comes San - ta Claus,   right down San - ta Claus Lane;

Vix - en and Blitz - en and all   his   rein - deer   pull - in'   on   the reins.____

"Frosty the Snowman" - Steve Nelson and Jack Rollins

Frost - y the snow-man was a jol - ly hap - py soul, with a

corn cob pipe and a but - ton nose—— and two eyes made out of coal.

Frost - y the snow-man is a fair - y tale they say. He was

"Rudolph, the Red-Nosed Reindeer" - Johnny Marks

Ru - dolph, the red - nosed rein - deer, had a ver - y shin - y nose.

You would e - ven say it

And if you ev - er saw him, you would e - ven say it glows.

glows.

He had a ver - y shin - y

Little Town

CHRIS EATON

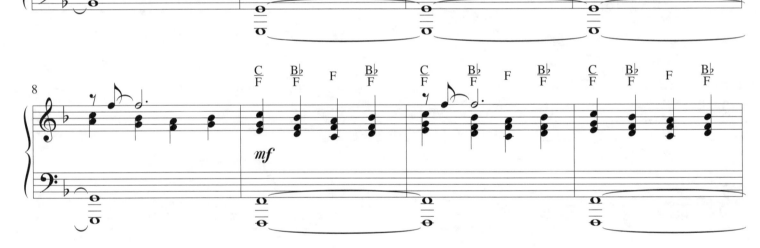

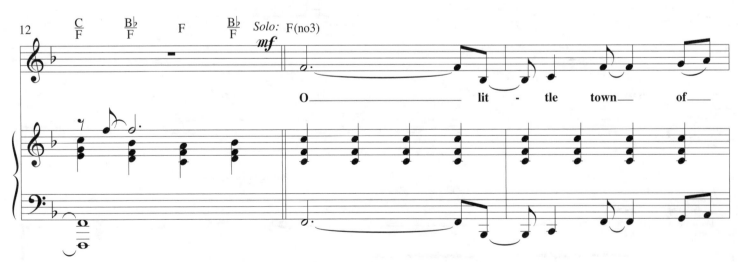

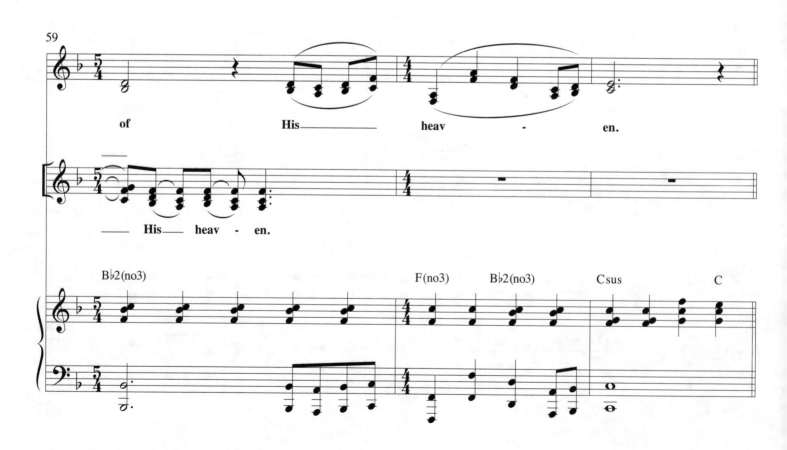

108

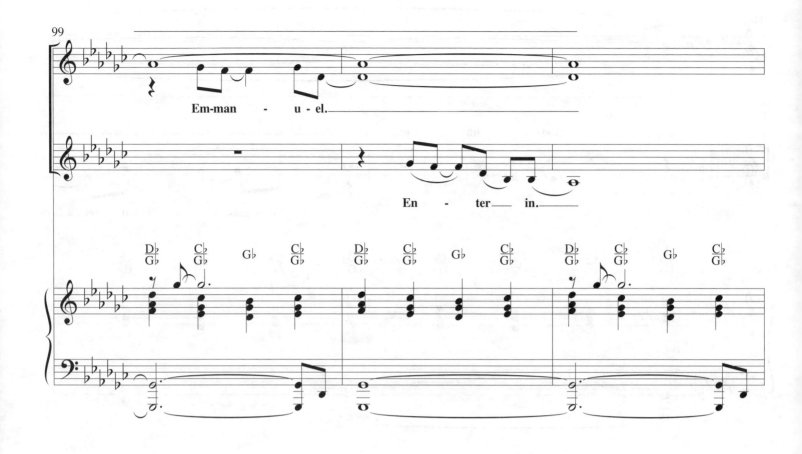

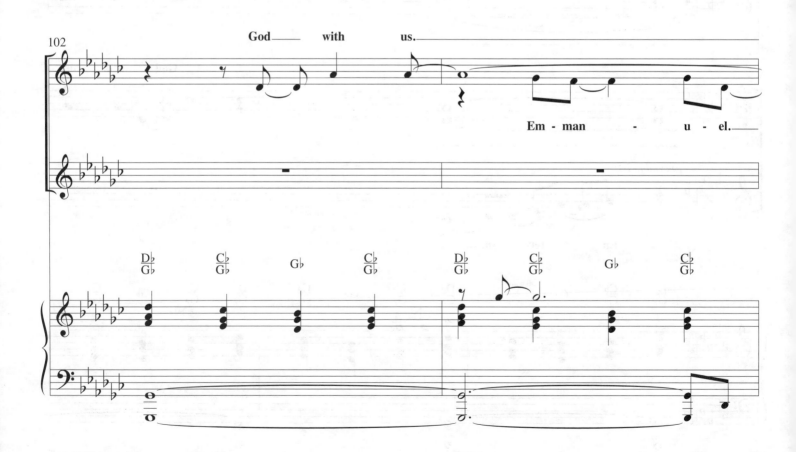

For unto Us

Based on the song by G. F. Handel
Arranged and new music by Carl Marsh

116

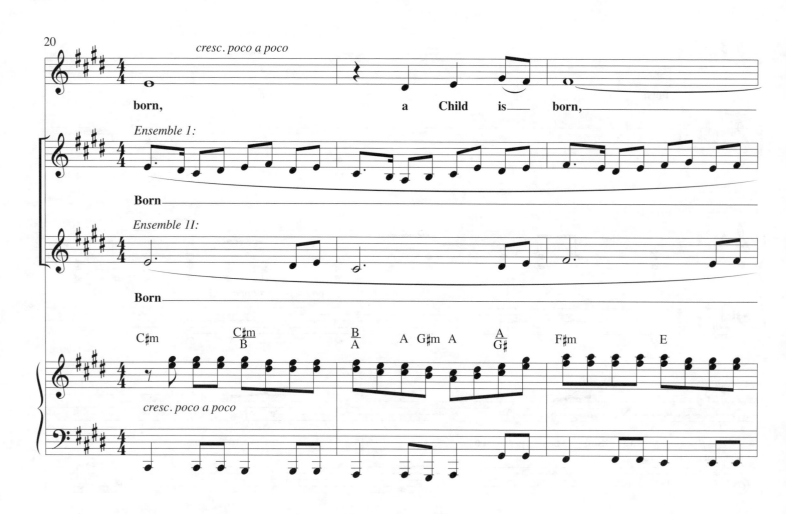

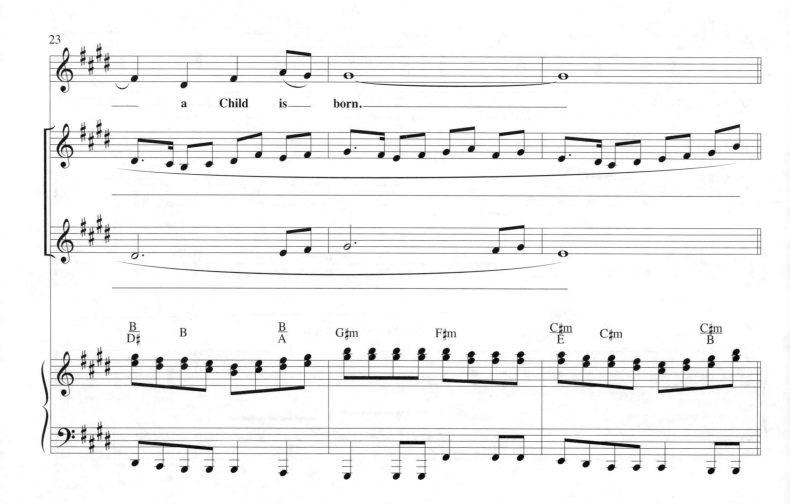

118

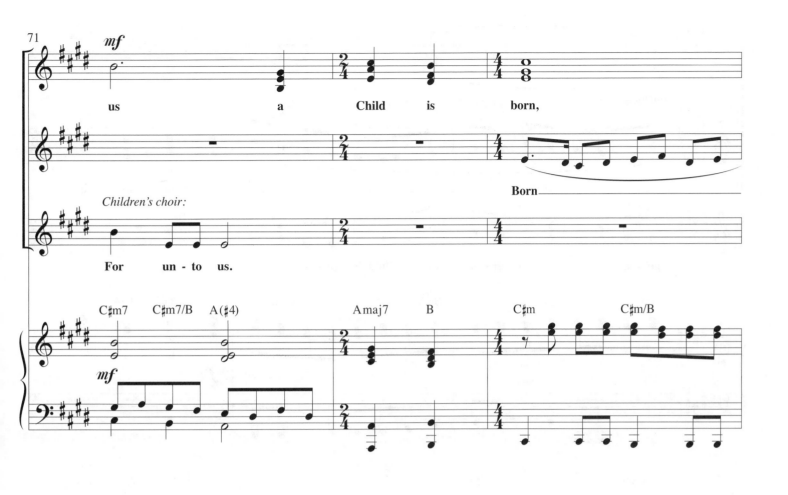

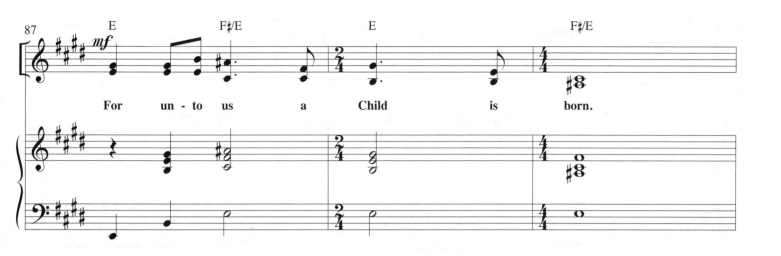

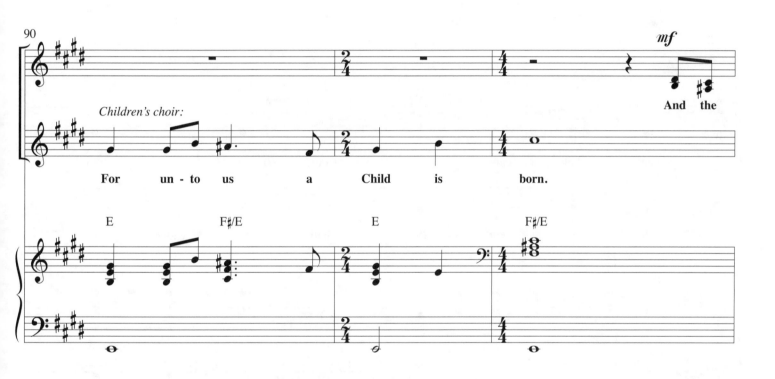

126

All Is Well

Words and Music by
MICHAEL W. SMITH
and WAYNE KIRKPATRICK

130